# Prayers That Avail Much®
## *for Graduates*

### James 5:16

*by*
*Germaine Copeland*

And this is the confidence that we have in him, that,
if we ask any thing according to his will, he heareth
us: and if we know that he hear us, whatsoever we
ask, we know that we have the petitions that we
desired of him.

1 John 5:14,15

**Harrison House**
Tulsa, Oklahoma

08 07 06 05 04      10 9 8 7 6 5 4 3 2 1

*Prayers That Avail Much® for Graduates*
Pocket Edition
ISBN 1-57794-644-8
Copyright © 2004 by Germaine Copeland
38 Sloan St.
Roswell, GA 30075

Published by Harrison House, Inc.
P.O. Box 35035
Tulsa, Oklahoma 74153

# *Contents*

## *Introduction*

You are living in a society that would lead you to believe that there are no absolutes — one in which everything you have been taught by the church is being challenged. Male and female roles are changing, family values are in the process of being redefined, and sensitivity to right and wrong is disappearing.

While educational textbooks, sociological theories, and philosophical reasoning are changing day by day, God's Word never changes. God remains true even when man's ideas, man's ways, fail. Jesus is the same yesterday, today, and forever (Heb. 13:8). God will never change (Mal. 3:6). He will never leave you without support (Heb. 13:5). He remains a trustworthy Friend, Savior, and Guide.

In His written Word, the heavenly Father has provided us values and guidelines for living. These instructions are absolutes. The Bible gives to us "the law of the Spirit of life in Christ Jesus" (Rom. 8:2) — a life that has promised abundance in every sphere of our existence. It is up to each individual to choose life or death, blessings or cursings (Deut. 30:19).

During these years of discovering who you are, resolve to decide your own convictions according to the Scriptures. Determine your identity, your integrity, your influence for good. Hide God's Word in your heart through Bible study and prayer. Determine how you will affect your world.

I am praying for you and believe that you will be all that God has created you to be, and that you will fulfill His plans and purposes for your life.

—Germaine Copeland, President
Word Ministries, Inc.

## *Personal Confessions*

Jesus is Lord over my spirit, my soul, and my body (Phil. 2:9-11).

Jesus has been made unto me wisdom, righteousness, sanctification, and redemption. I can do all things through Christ Who strengthens me (1 Cor. 1:30; Phil. 4:13).

The Lord is my shepherd. I do not want. My God supplies all my need according to His riches in glory in Christ Jesus (Ps. 23; Phil. 4:19).

I do not fret or have anxiety about anything. I do not have a care (Phil. 4:6; 1 Pet. 5:6,7).

I am the Body of Christ. I am redeemed from the curse, because Jesus bore my sicknesses and carried my diseases in His own body. By His stripes I am healed. I forbid any sickness or disease to operate in my body. Every organ and tissue of my body functions in the perfection in which God created it to function. I honor God and bring glory to Him in my body (Gal. 3:13, Matt. 8:17; 1 Pet. 2:24; 1 Cor. 6:20).

I have the mind of Christ and hold the thoughts, feelings, and purposes of His heart (1 Cor. 2:16).

I am a believer and not a doubter. I hold fast to my confession of faith. I decide to walk by faith and practice faith. My faith comes by hearing and hearing by the Word of God. Jesus is the author and the developer of my faith (Heb. 4:14; Heb. 11:6; Rom. 10:17; Heb. 12:2).

The Holy Spirit has shed the love of God abroad in my heart, and His love abides in me richly. I keep myself in the Kingdom of light, in love, in the Word; and the wicked one touches me not (Rom. 5:5; 1 John 4:16; 1 John 5:18).

I tread upon serpents and scorpions and over all the power of the enemy. I take my shield of faith and quench his every fiery dart. Greater is He Who is in me than he who is in the world (Ps. 91:13; Eph. 6:16; 1 John 4:4).

I am delivered from this present evil world. I am seated with Christ in heavenly places. I reside in the Kingdom of God's dear Son. The and bring glory to Him in my body (Gal. 3:13; Matt. 8:17; 1 Pet. 2:24; 1 Cor. 6:20).

I have the mind of Christ and hold the thoughts, feelings, and purposes of His heart (1 Cor. 2:16).

I am a believer and not a doubter. I hold fast to my confession of faith. I decide to walk by faith and practice faith. My faith comes by hearing and hearing by the Word of God. Jesus is the author and the developer of my faith (Heb. 4:14; Heb. 11:6; Rom. 10:17; Heb. 12:2).

The Holy Spirit has shed the love of God abroad in my heart, and His love abides in me richly. I keep myself in the Kingdom of light, in love, in the Word; and the wicked one touches me not (Rom. 5:5; 1 John 4:16; 1 John 5:18).

I tread upon serpents and scorpions and over all the power of the enemy. I take my shield of faith and quench his every fiery dart. Greater is He Who is in me than he who is in the world (Ps. 91:13; Eph. 6:16; 1 John 4:4).

I am delivered from this present evil world. I am seated with Christ in heavenly places. I reside in the Kingdom of God's dear Son. The

# 1
## *To Walk in the Word*

Father, in the name of Jesus, I commit myself to walk in the Word. Your Word living in me produces Your life in this world. I recognize that Your Word is integrity itself, and I trust my life to its provisions.

You have sent Your Word forth into my heart. It dwells in me richly in all wisdom. I meditate in it day and night so that I may diligently act on it. The Incorruptible Seed is abiding in my spirit, growing mightily in me now, producing Your nature, Your life. It is my counsel, my shield, my buckler, my powerful weapon in battle. The Word is a lamp to my feet and a light to my path, making my way plain before me. I do not stumble, for my steps are ordered in the Word.

The Holy Spirit leads and guides me into all the truth, giving me understanding, discernment, and comprehension so that I am preserved from the snares of the evil one.

I delight myself in You and Your Word, and You put Your desires within my heart. I commit my way unto You, and You make me successful. You are working in me now, giving me the power and desire to do all Your will.

I exalt Your Word, hold it in high esteem, and give it first place. I make my schedule around Your Word, making the Word the final authority to settle all questions that confront me. I agree with the Word of God, and disagree with any thoughts, attitudes, or circumstances contrary to Your Word. I boldly and confidently say that my heart is fixed and established on the solid foundation — the living Word of God!

---

### Scripture References

| | |
|---|---|
| Psalms 37:4,5,23; 91:4; 112:7,8; 119:105 | John 16:13 |
| | Ephesians 6:10 |
| Hebrews 4:12 | Luke 18:1 |
| Colossians 1:9; 3:16; 4:2 | Philippians 2:13 |
| Joshua 1:8 | 2 Corinthians 10:5 |
| 1 Peter 1:23; 3:12 | |

## 2

## *Commitment to the Lord*

Father, I pray that Your plan for my life will be fulfilled. My number one priority is to submit myself in love to You. I embrace Your truth rather than the basic principles of this world. I will not be conformed to the pattern of this world, but I ask to be transformed by the renewing of my mind. Then I will be able to test and approve what Your will is for me. I believe in Your Word, which is Your expressed will for my life.

Father, I purpose to obey You and remain in Your love. I love others and will show them by my actions. I commit and dedicate my whole body, mind, and spirit to You. I will serve You, my God, and keep Your commandments.

I will not follow the voice of a stranger. I choose my companions and friends carefully, according to Your Word, and determine to walk in paths of righteousness for Your name's sake.

Thank You that You chose me — actually picked me out for Yourself as Your own child — to be holy and blameless in Your sight.

I have made the decision to follow You as long as I live. I trust You to lead me and guide me through Your Word with the Holy Spirit as my Helper. I commit and trust my works to You — so that You cause my plans to be established and succeed. In Jesus' name I pray. Amen.

### Scripture References

Psalm 23:3 AMP

Psalms 37:4,5; 42:1

Proverbs 16:3 AMP

Jeremiah 29:13; 42:6

Lamentations 3:25

Luke 10:27

John 10:5 KJV; 14:16 AMP

Acts 17:24,27,28

Romans 8:14,26; 12:2

1 Corinthians 15:33 AMP

Ephesians 1:4 AMP

Colossians 1:9; 2:20-22; 3:1-3

## 3
## *Praise and Thanksgiving*

Father, I love You and praise You. I thank You for Your goodness and Your love. I'll continually thank You for Your mercy, which endures forever.

I praise You, Lord, and I will not forget all Your benefits. Thank You for forgiving my sins and for healing all my diseases. You fill my life with good things.

Father, You created the heavens, the earth, the sea, and everything in them. Thank You for making me so I can enjoy life to the fullest. This is the day that You have made, and I rejoice and I am glad in it. You are my strength and my joy.

I thank You and praise You for supplying and providing everything I need. You are all-powerful, You know everything, and You are everywhere. Thank You for being such a loving

Father to me that You gave Jesus to be my
Savior, Lord, and Friend. Thank You for sending
the Holy Spirit to fill me, guide me, comfort me,
and teach me the right things to do.

I'll praise You in everything.

In Jesus' name I pray. Amen.

-------

### *Scripture References*

Psalms 18:30; 24:1; 28:7;      Nehemiah 8:10
  34:1; 48:1; 63:3,4,5;      John 10:10 KJV; 14:16 AMP
  71:8; 103:2,3,5,8;      Philippians 4:19
  106:1; 118:24; 136:1      Revelation 4:8,11

## 4
## *Wisdom and God's Will*

Heavenly Father, may I be filled with the clear knowledge of Your will in all wisdom and understanding. I know that Your will and Your Word agree. I will continue to meditate on Your Word so I can know Your plan and Your purpose for this season in my life. I want to live in a way that is worthy of You and fully pleasing to You. I believe You will cause my thoughts to agree with Your will so that I may be fruitful in every good work.

Your wisdom is pure and full of compassion. Teach me to love. I am growing strong in faith. Your words contain a wealth of wisdom.

As for this situation today, I thank You for Your wisdom in knowing the right thing to do and to say. I have decided to listen to You. Teach me the way that You want me to go. Thank You for counseling me and watching carefully over me. Thank You for the Holy Spirit; He is my Teacher, Helper, and Guide. I believe He is active in my life.

I won't be afraid or confused, because Your Word brings me light and understanding. Although there are many voices in the world, I will follow the voice of my Shepherd.

Thank You for the wise parents, teachers, and pastors You have put in my life to teach and instruct me. I will seek godly counsel from them. When I need to make an important, final decision, I will follow the peace that comes from knowing Your Word.

I dedicate everything I do to You, knowing that my plans will succeed. I trust You with my life and everything in it. I thank You that to follow after You is to follow after peace in my heart. I thank You for Your wisdom. In Jesus' name I pray. Amen.

### Scripture References

Psalms 16:7; 32:8;
118:8; 119:99,130,133

Proverbs 2:6; 6:20-23;
19:21

Proverbs 16:3,9 AMP

Joshua 1:9

John 10:15

1 Corinthians 14:33

Ephesians 5:15

Colossians 1:9; 3:16

James 1:5,6; 3:17

1 John 5:14,15

## 5

## *The Setting of Proper Priorities*

Father, I ask You to help me establish priorities. I confess my weakness of procrastination and lack of organization. I desire to live purposefully, worthily, and accurately as a wise, sensible, intelligent person.

You have given me a seven-day week: six days to work and the seventh to rest. Help me make the most of the time [buying up each opportunity]. Help me plan my day and stay focused on my assignments.

In the name of Jesus, I smash warped philosophies, tear down barriers erected against the truth of God, and fit every loose thought, emotion, and impulse into the structure of life shaped by Christ. I clear my mind of every obstruction and build a life of obedience into maturity.

Father, I plan the way I want to live — organizing my efforts, scheduling my activities, and budgeting my time — but You alone enable me to live it. Jesus, You want me to relax, to not be preoccupied with getting, so I can respond to God's giving. I know You, Father God, and how You work. I steep my life in God-reality, God-initiative, and God-provisions.

Father, Your Word shows me my life as complete in Christ. I cast all my cares, worries, and concerns on You, that I might be well-balanced (temperate, sober of mind), vigilant, and cautious at all times. I tune my ears to the word of wisdom, set my heart on a life of understanding, and make insight my priority.

Father, You sent Jesus that I might know You and have life more abundantly. Help me remember that my relationships with You and others are more important than anything else. Amen.

### Scripture References

Ephesians 5:15,16 AMP

2 Corinthians 10:5,6
  MESSAGE

Matthew 11:29; 6:31-33
  MESSAGE

Matthew 11:29 AMP

Proverbs 2:2,3; 16:3,9
  MESSAGE

Colossians 2:10

Genesis 2:2 NIV

1 Peter 5:7,8 AMP

John 10:10

# 6

## *Protection*

Father, You are my stronghold and my
fortress. You are my God; in You will I trust. I
will not be afraid of any terror by day or night,
for You are always with me.

Lord, You are a shield about me to protect
me. You are my light and my salvation — whom
shall I fear? You are the stronghold of my life —
of whom shall I be afraid? When evil men come
to destroy me, they will stumble and fall!

I have peace in my heart because perfect love
casts out all fear. You have not given me a
spirit of fear, but of power and of love and of a
sound mind.

Your Word promises me that no evil will come
upon me, no accident will overtake me, and no
disease or tragedy will come near my home. No
weapon aimed at me will succeed. So I am

strong, courageous, and fearless. Thank You for angels to keep me safe in all that I do.

Father, You have promised Your children a sweet, peaceful sleep, so I thank You that I can rest at night free from fear or nightmares. You give me peace and rest; Jesus is my safety. Thank You for protecting me.

In Jesus' name I pray. Amen.

*To remind yourself of God's protection,*
*read Psalm 91 and Psalm 23 often.*

---

### Scripture References

Psalms 3:3; 4:8; 23:4; 27:1,2; 91:5,9-12

Psalm 34:7 AMP

Isaiah 54:17

2 Timothy 1:7

1 John 3:8; 4:18

# 7
## *Healing*

I come to Your throne boldly in faith to
receive my healing. I confess Your Word,
believing that Your Word will not return to You
void, but will accomplish what it says it will.
Thank You for Jesus, Who took my sicknesses
and carried away my diseases. Because of the
stripes on Jesus' back, I believe that I am healed.

Jesus saved me from the curse of sickness. I
have confidence in the Word, which abides in
me, to heal me. I have on the whole armor of
God, and the shield of faith protects me from
all the fiery darts of the wicked one.

Healing is the children's bread, and I am Your
child, so I receive total and complete healing for
my body and mind. My faith is based on Jesus,
the Word of God. Your Word is health, life, and
medicine to my whole body.

Father, Your Word says that my tongue has the power of life and death; therefore, I speak words filled with faith, hope, life, and health. I stand delivered to perfect soundness of mind and wholeness in body and spirit from the deepest parts of my nature in my immortal spirit even to the joints and marrow of my bones.

In Jesus' name I pray. Amen.

---

### Scripture References

Proverbs 3:8; 4:20-22; 18:21

Exodus 15:26

Psalms 91:2; 103:3; 107:2

Isaiah 53:5; 55:11

Matthew 18:18

Mark 7:27

Galatians 3:13

Ephesians 6:11,16

Hebrews 4:12,16

John 1:14

1 Peter 2:24

Acts 10:38

## 8

# *Victory in a Healthy Lifestyle*

Father, I am Your child and Jesus is Lord over my spirit, soul, and body. I praise You because I am fearfully and wonderfully made. Your works are wonderful; I know that full well.

Lord, thank You for declaring Your plans for me — plans to prosper me and not to harm me, plans to give me hope and a future. I choose to renew my mind to Your plans for a healthy lifestyle. You have abounded toward me in all prudence and wisdom. Therefore, I give thought to my steps and to what I eat. Teach me knowledge and good judgment that I might attain and maintain the proper body weight.

My body is for the Lord. So here's what I want to do with Your help, Father God. I choose to take my everyday, ordinary life — my sleeping, eating, going-to-work, and walking-around life — and place it before You as an offering. Embracing what You do for me is the best thing I can do for You.

Christ the Messiah is magnified and receives glory and praise in this body of mine, and He is boldly exalted in my person. Thank You, Father, in Jesus' name! Hallelujah! Amen.

_____

### Scripture References

Psalms 119:66; 139:14          Romans 12:1 MESSAGE

Jeremiah 29:11                       Philippians 1:20 AMP

Proverbs 14:15

## 9

## *Finances*

Father, thank You for being my Source of everything that is good. Before I even ask, You know my financial needs. You said that the things I desire (in accordance with Your will) will be given to me if I ask You. Because I trust You, I ask specifically for $_____ to meet my present financial need.

Thank You for jobs, parents, friends, or associates who bless me financially. I cherish and respect them, but I recognize You as my Source. I won't worry, because I have You to provide for my every financial need. Your Word says that You take pleasure in the prosperity of Your servant.

Because You have given me the ability to obtain wealth, I will look for good ideas and opportunities to earn the money that I need. I will keep a good attitude and work hard. Thank You for giving me favor with others.

Your Word promises that since I have given my tithes and offerings to You cheerfully, without complaining, I will always have enough. I will stay faithful and thankful to You and to the people You use to meet my needs. Because I am Your child, I believe You will bless those who bless me.

Please help me to learn to handle my money wisely. Thank You for meeting my financial needs so that I can prosper and enjoy life to the fullest.

In Jesus' name I pray. Amen.

---

### Scripture References

Genesis 12:2,3

Numbers 23:19

Deuteronomy 8:18;
    28:1-13

Psalms 23:1; 34:10;
    35:27

Proverbs 3:4,9,10; 10:4

Ecclesiastes 5:19

Isaiah 65:24

Malachi 3:10,11

Matthew 6:32,33

Luke 6:38

2 Corinthians 9:7

Philippians 4:19

James 1:17

1 John 5:14,15

# 10

# *Controlling Your Thoughts/ Renewing Your Mind*

Father, You know all of my thoughts and the attitudes of my heart. May my spoken words and unspoken thoughts be pleasing in Your sight, O Lord, my Rock and my Redeemer.

You gave me Your Word as a weapon to fight impure and unholy thoughts. Your Word is alive and more powerful than any weapon known to man, able to pull down all evil strongholds.

I will concentrate on truth, goodness, and righteousness. I will think about things that are pure and lovely, and dwell on the good attributes in others. I will think about all that I can praise You for and be glad about.

I thank You for giving me the helmet of salvation to guard my mind. As I commit to stay in Your Word daily, I will begin to think more and more like You, Father. I will diligently guard my mind and heart by not allowing unhealthy thoughts to control me.

Thank You for giving me the mind of Christ. Help me to make all my thoughts obedient to Jesus, the Word.

In Jesus' name I pray. Amen.

---

### Scripture References

Psalms 19:14 TLB; 94:11; 139:2-4,23

Proverbs 4:23

Isaiah 26:3; 55:8,9

1 Corinthians 2:16

2 Corinthians 10:3-5

Ephesians 6:17

Philippians 4:6-8

Colossians 3:2

Hebrews 4:12

## 11
## *Controlling Your Tongue*

Father, Your Word says, "He who has knowledge spares his words, and a man of understanding has a cool spirit. Even a fool when he holds his peace is considered wise; when he closes his lips he is esteemed a man of understanding" (Prov. 17:27,28 AMP). Proverbs 29:20 (KJV) says, "Seest thou a man that is hasty in his words? there is more hope of a fool than of him." And James 3:2 (KJV) says, "For in many things we offend all. If any man offend not in word, the same is a perfect man, and able also to bridle the whole body."

Lord, You have said that life and death are in the power of the tongue, and that the fruit of my lips will satisfy me. Out of the abundance of my heart, my mouth speaks. I will feed my spirit Your Word so that Your Word will be abundant in me.

Father, Your words are life to those who find them and health to all their flesh. When I speak Your Word, it produces life and health in me. I believe that I can control what I say because no unique or new temptations come to me; You are faithful to make a way of escape from the temptation to sin with my mouth. Father, I will learn to be quick to hear and slow to speak.

Jesus said that I would be judged for all empty and idle words. I can either speak words of love, faith, and hope; or words of doubt, unbelief, and hate. Father, I choose to speak Your Word of life, peace, joy, and faith.

Good words are sweet to hear and bring life. Help me always to be someone who says good things. Thank You, Father, for a pure heart and pure words. In Jesus' name I pray. Amen.

---

### Scripture References

Proverbs 4:20-22; 10:19;    1 Corinthians 10:13 AMP
   16:24; 17:9; 18:21      Ephesians 4:25,29
Matthew 5:8; 12:34       James 1:19; 4:11
Matthew 12:36 TLB

## 12
## *Confession: "I Am God's Child"*

Behold what manner of love the Father has bestowed upon me, that I should be called a son/daughter of God.

Thank You for choosing me — for appointing me — that I might go and bear fruit and keep on bearing; that my fruit may be lasting. I have received and welcomed Jesus and stand in the power and authority to become a child of God.

Father, I am led by Your Spirit; therefore, I am Your child. I have not received the spirit of bondage again to fear; but I have received the Spirit of adoption, whereby I cry, "Abba! Father!" The Spirit itself bears witness with my spirit, that I am a child of God. And since I am Your child, I am an heir: an heir of God and a joint-heir with Christ.

Father, I will not be unequally yoked together with unbelievers, for I am the temple of the living God. You dwell in me and walk in me; You are my God, and I am Your child. I come out from among the world, and I will be separate. I will not touch the unclean thing; therefore, You receive me as Your child.

I rejoice, Father, because You have said, "...I will receive you, and will be a Father unto you, and ye shall be my sons and daughters..." (2 Cor. 6:16,17). You are the Lord Almighty, and there has not failed one word of all Your good promise.

Today I am a child of God —
A God Who sees, a God Who hears,
A God Who watches over me.
Today I am a child of God.

---

### Scripture References

1 Kings 8:56

John 1:12; 15:16 AMP

John 17:11,16

2 Corinthians 6:14-18

1 John 3:1

## 13
# *Finding Favor With Others*

### *A Prayer of Intercession*

Father, in the name of Jesus, You make Your face to shine upon and enlighten _____ and are gracious (kind, merciful, and giving favor) to him/her. _____ is the head and not the tail. _____ is above only and not beneath.

Thank You for favor for _____, who seeks Your Kingdom and Your righteousness and diligently seeks good. _____ is a blessing to You, Lord, and is a blessing to *(name them: family, neighbors, business associates, etc.).* Grace (favor) is with _____, who loves the Lord Jesus in sincerity. _____ extends favor, honor, and love to *(names).* _____ is flowing in Your love, Father. You are pouring out upon _____ the spirit of favor. You crown him/her with glory and honor, for he/she is Your child — Your workmanship.

_____ is a success today. _____ is someone very special with You, Lord.

_____ is growing in the Lord — waxing strong in spirit. Father, You give _____ knowledge and skill in all learning and wisdom.

You bring _____ to find favor, compassion, and loving-kindness with _____ *(names)*. _____ obtains favor in the sight of all who look upon him/her this day, in the name of Jesus. _____ is filled with Your fullness — rooted and grounded in love. You are doing exceeding abundantly above all that _____ asks or thinks, for Your mighty power is taking over in _____.

Thank You, Father, that _____ is well-favored by You and by man, in Jesus' name!

---

### Scripture References

| | |
|---|---|
| Numbers 6:25 | Luke 6:38 |
| Deuteronomy 28:13 | Zechariah 12:10 |
| Matthew 6:33 | Psalm 8:5 |
| Proverbs 11:27 | Luke 2:40 |
| Ephesians 2:10; 3:19,20; | Daniel 1:9,17 |
|    6:24 | Esther 2:15,17 |

## 14

## *Your Appearance*

Father, Your Word says that You knitted me together in my mother's womb. My frame was not hidden from You when I was being formed in secret [and] intricately and curiously wrought [as if embroidered with various colors].

I know that Jesus came so that I could enjoy life to its fullest. I speak Your words of life to myself. I will spend time developing a quiet and meek spirit. I know that my outward appearance is also important to You, for You care about every area of my life. You give me the desires of my heart when I delight myself in You and commit my ways to You.

I accept and feel good about myself, so that I am confident and present myself well. Help me to learn how to take care of myself and to maximize all the natural gifts that You gave me when You created me. Help me to listen to the Holy Spirit, the Teacher inside of me, keeping in mind that my body is His temple. I will control and discipline my body. I believe that with Your help, I can lose weight, or add and tone muscles, to maximize the physical beauty of the body that You gave me.

Father, help me to exercise consistently and take care of this temple of the Holy Spirit. Help me to be patient and to change any lifestyle or eating habits that might be destructive. Your Word is life to me and health to all my flesh.

I thank You for the beauty of a godly character. I treat my body with respect because Your Holy Spirit lives in me. I am so valuable that You gave Your only Son for my salvation. I believe that You are still perfecting everything that involves me, including the way I look. In Jesus' name I pray. Amen.

---

### Scripture References

Psalms 37:4,5; 100:3; 138:8; 149:4

Psalm 139:13,15 AMP

Genesis 1:26,27,31

Proverbs 4:20-22; 31:30

Isaiah 44:2

John 3:16; 10:10

1 Corinthians 6:19,20

1 Corinthians 9:25-27 AMP

1 Peter 3:4; 5:7

## 15
## *Self-Esteem*

Father, I come to Your throne room in order to receive help for my self-image. You created me in Your image and likeness, and that means so much to me. I know that You always love me. I know You didn't just carelessly or thoughtlessly throw me together. You made me so wonderfully complex! It is amazing to think about. Your workmanship is marvelous — and how well I know it.

Because I am Your workmanship, Your handicraft, made for good works, I ask You to help me to view myself from Your perspective. Help me to realize my strengths. Open my eyes to the strengths, abilities, and talents that You have placed inside of me. Give me grace to find the good that is in me. Help me to be appreciative of who I am, instead of critical of who I am not.

Although the world places importance on physical appearance, Father, I know that You judge the heart. You are interested in a pure heart and a humble spirit. I know that I am very valuable to You. Knowing that I am chosen makes me feel special. Thank You for choosing me before the foundation of the world. I acknowledge You, God, as my Father, and thank You that I am Your child.

Help me to set my affections on things above rather than on things of the world. Help me to mature in my relationship with You and to develop into the happy, joyful, strong Christian that I have the potential to be.

In Jesus' name I pray. Amen.

---

### Scripture References

| | |
|---|---|
| Genesis 1:27 | Ephesians 1:4 KJV; 2:10 AMP |
| 1 Samuel 16:7 | Colossians 3:2 |
| Psalm 139:14 | Hebrews 4:16 |
| Isaiah 57:15 | 1 Peter 2:9; 4:10 |
| Romans 12:1 | 1 John 3:1-3 |
| 2 Corinthians 6:18 | |

## 16
## *Meeting New Friends*

Father, I come boldly to Your throne to ask You to help me to meet some new friends. I know that You are the source of love and friendship, but You also desire to express Your love and friendship toward me through others. So I am convinced that it is Your will for me to have godly friendships with members of both sexes.

Your Word reveals the purpose and value of healthy friendships. It is not the quantity, but the quality, of friends that matters.

Holy Spirit, teach me what I need to know to be a quality friend. Help me to show myself friendly to others and to love my friends at all times.

I purpose to live in peace as much as is possible, and pray that when my friends and I come together we will encourage each other. Help me to rid myself of any prejudice or partiality. I will not [attempt to] hold [and] practice the faith of our Lord Jesus Christ [the Lord] of glory [together with snobbery]! I will welcome and receive others as You, Father, have received me.

Help me to be kind, humble, and gentle. Help me to forgive those who need forgiveness, because I am forgiven. For my new friends, I thank You.

In Jesus' name I pray. Amen.

---

### Scripture References

Psalm 84:11

Proverbs 13:20; 17:17

Ecclesiastes 4:9,10

John 15:13

Romans 15:7 AMP

1 Corinthians 1:10

Ephesians 4:2,32 AMP

Philippians 1:27; 2:2

Colossians 2:2

Hebrews 4:16

James 1:17 KJV; 2:1 AMP

## 17
## *Boldness*

Father, help me to be bolder. Help me not to confuse boldness with being loud, obnoxious, or rude, but to recognize that true boldness comes from knowing that I know that I abide in Jesus and that Jesus and His Word abide in me. Boldness comes not by might nor by power, but by Your Spirit.

Father, I want to be bold with my love just as Jesus was bold with His love. I desire a quiet confidence and assurance that come from knowing You. Please give me the wisdom to know when to be quiet and when to speak out. Open my eyes so that I can see people as Jesus sees them. Thank You for giving me a heart of compassion and love for everyone.

I am not ashamed of You, Father, and I am not ashamed of the Gospel of Jesus Christ. Because I really love people, I am not afraid to tell them about Jesus. Thank You for giving me the words to say, so that when I talk to others, it is like You, God, talking to them. I will live in an exemplary manner representing You by both my words and my actions. My behavior will reflect love, joy, and peace to others.

I thank You that I am not hindered by fear, because You have not given me a spirit of fear, but of power and of love and of a sound mind. I know that perfect love casts out all fear. So by faith, I believe that I will not be intimidated by what other people think or say or do.

Thank You for courage and strength to love and to live like Jesus. I am asking You for boldness, wisdom, and freedom to declare Your message fearlessly at just the right time to my friends at school and at work.

In Jesus' name I pray. Amen.

### *Scripture References*

Proverbs 28:1

Zechariah 4:6

Matthew 10:19,20;
  16:15,16

John 15:7,8

Acts 4:13,29,33

Romans 1:16; 5:5

2 Corinthians 4:4-6

Ephesians 6:19

2 Timothy 1:7

Hebrews 13:6

James 1:5

1 Peter 4:11

1 John 4:18

## 18
## *Before a Vacation or a Road Trip*

Father, I set my expectations and hopes upon You because You generously provide me with everything for my enjoyment. I look to You to fill me with Your joy and peace as we have fun, excitement, laughter, and adventure on this vacation/road trip. I cast all my cares upon You right now. I refuse to worry or fret about anything.

Please lead and guide me, and speak to my heart during this time away. Help me to meet and to make new friends while we travel. Make me a blessing to others and use me as a witness to those I meet who don't know You. Grant me words of life to speak to their hearts so they can be born again.

As I travel, grant me eyes to see, ears to hear, and a heart to appreciate all of Your wonderful creation. Please show me those secret things that You share only with those who fear and respect You.

Thank You for granting me wisdom to handle every situation. Help me to travel intelligently and to act in a manner that is pleasing to You.

Thank You for giving Your angels charge over me to keep me in all my ways. They will bear me up in their hands and encamp all around me to protect me from all harm or evil. Thank You that You protect not only my physical body, but also all of my property. Thank You, Father, that the transportation vehicle will be safe and operate perfectly without problems.

I will be sure to spend time in Your Word and in prayer while I am away, and to go to church if the opportunity arises. I thank You that we will have excellent weather, and that this will be a fun, safe, exciting, and adventurous vacation/road trip filled with laughter, rest, and relaxation — so that I can return refreshed and rejuvenated.

In Jesus' name I pray. Amen.

### Scripture References

Psalms 25:14; 34:7;
   91:10-12; 127:2

Psalm 23:2,3 AMP

Isaiah 54:17

Matthew 11:28

Acts 3:19 AMP

Romans 15:13

Philippians 4:6,7

1 Timothy 6:17

James 3:5

1 Peter 5:7

# 19
## *To Help Others*

Father, in the name of Jesus, I purpose to do unto others as I would have them do unto me. I eagerly pursue and seek to acquire [this] (agape) love — I make it my aim, my great quest in life.

In the name of Jesus, I will esteem and look upon and be concerned for not [merely] my own interest, but also for the interest of others as they pursue success. I am strong in the Lord, and in the power of Your might. I will make it a practice to please (make happy) my neighbor, (boss, co-worker, teacher, parent, child, brother, etc.) for his good and for his true welfare, to edify him — that is, to strengthen him and build him up in all ways — spiritually, socially, and materially.

I desire to imitate my Heavenly Father, and as a child of light, I will walk in love and wisdom.

Help me to encourage (admonish, exhort) others and edify them.

Father, in the name of Jesus, I love my enemies (as well as my business associates, fellow church members, neighbors, those in authority over me) and am kind and do good — doing favors so that someone derives benefit from them. I lend expecting and hoping for nothing in return, but considering nothing as lost and despairing of no one.

Thank You, Father, for imprinting Your laws upon my heart, and inscribing them on my mind — on my inmost thoughts and understanding. According to Your Word, as I would like and desire that men would do to me, I do exactly so to them, in the name of Jesus.

---

### Scripture References

| | |
|---|---|
| Luke 6:31 KJV, AMP | Romans 15:2 AMP |
| 1 Corinthians 14:1 AMP | 1 Thessalonians 5:11 AMP |
| Philippians 2:4 AMP | Luke 6:35,36 AMP |
| Ephesians 5:1,2 AMP; 6:10 | Hebrews 10:16 AMP |

## 20
## *Equipped for Success*

Father, thank You that the entrance of Your words gives light. Your Word is alive and powerful, giving me a spirit of power, love, and a calm and well-balanced mind, discipline, and self-control. You have qualified me as a minister of a new covenant. In Jesus' name, I walk out of the realm of failure into the arena of success, giving thanks to You for qualifying me to share the inheritance of the saints in the Light.

I praise You, Father, for giving me every blessing in heaven because I belong to Christ. You have given me all I need for life and godliness through my knowledge of Him Who called me by His own glory and goodness. I rejoice in Jesus, Who has given me abundant life. I am a new creation, for I am (engrafted) in Christ. The old has passed away. Behold, the fresh and new has come! I forget what is behind and reach for what is before me. I am crucified with Christ: nevertheless I live; yet not I, but Christ lives in me: and I live by the faith of the Son, Who loved me and gave Himself for me.

Father, I attend, consent, and submit to Your sayings. I will keep Your words in the center of my heart. They are life *(success)* to me, healing and health to all my flesh. I keep and guard my heart above all, for out of it flow the springs of life. I will not let mercy, kindness, and truth forsake me. I bind them about my neck; I write them upon the tablet of my heart. Therefore, I will find favor, good understanding, and high esteem in the sight of God and man.

Father, my delight and desire are in Your Law, and on it I habitually meditate (ponder and study) day and night. I am like a tree planted by the streams of water, ready to bring forth fruit in my season; my leaf shall not wither, and everything I do shall prosper. *Now thanks be unto God, which always causeth us to triumph in Christ!*

### *Scripture References*

2 Corinthians 2:14

2 Corinthians 3:5;
5:17 AMP

Psalms 1:2,3 AMP;
119:130

Proverbs 3:3,4;
4:20-23 AMP

Hebrews 4:12 AMP

2 Timothy 1:7 AMP

Colossians 1:12,13 AMP

Ephesians 1:3 TLB

John 10:10 AMP

Philippians 3:13

Galatians 2:20

2 Peter 1:3 NIV

## 21
## *Part-Time or Full-Time Job*

Father, thank You that You are my Provider and my Source of total supply. Every good thing that I have comes from You. I believe You will show me a way to earn and manage my money.

Thank You that I am happy where I work, enjoying the results of my labor. You are leading me to the best possible job — one that will not conflict with my relationship with You, or with any of my family, school, or church priorities.

With Your help I will not grow tired of doing what is right, but will develop a strong work ethic and have an excellent and enthusiastic attitude. Help me to be obedient to my employer. If something goes against my conscience, give me the words to communicate my objection in a clear and concise manner. Thank You for giving me favor with those who can change things without making a bad scene.

Help me to be an effective witness for the Gospel by working hard, diligently, and quietly with a humble spirit at all times, not just when my boss is around, but as if I were working for You, because I am working for You.

Father, I am strong in You and the power of Your might. I will not give up, but trust that my work will be recognized and rewarded. Thank You for Your protection so I don't have to be nervous or afraid of anything, but I share my requests with You in prayer. Thanks for Your peace that protects my heart and mind in every situation.

Father, please help me to have absolute and complete control over my tongue, what I say, so that I won't hurt or offend anyone. I won't murmur, complain, backbite, or gossip.

Thank You that I have favor with my boss and with all of the people I work with. In Jesus' name I pray. Amen.

---

### *Scripture References*

Deuteronomy 8:18

2 Chronicles 15:7

Proverbs 11:27 AMP

Ecclesiastes 5:18-20

Isaiah 48:17

John 6:43

1 Corinthians 15:58

Ephesians 6:5-7

Philippians 4:6,7,19

Colossians 3:23,24

1 Thessalonians 4:11,12

2 Thessalonians 3:13

James 1:5,17; 3:2

## 22

## *Your Future*

Father, I am dedicated to live for You. I don't know everything the future holds for me, but I know that it is in Your hands. I trust You to lead me, to be my guide in life. Thank You for preparing me now for Your life plan for me, and for giving me the wisdom to discern the right timing for what You would have me do in each season of my life. I choose to love, obey, and cleave unto You with my whole body, soul, and spirit.

Help me to recognize the skills You have given me so that I can develop them and give the glory to You. Give me understanding and light so that I am quick to learn. I thank You for the wisdom and light that come from You and Your Word.

You are a help to me in everything I do. If it is Your will for me to marry someday, I thank

You that You are not only preparing me, but that You are also working on my future spouse. Until that time comes, help me to be content in every situation.

I believe that You will supply all the money I need to do Your will. I believe You will instruct me and teach me which way to go. You don't make things confusing for me, but You make a clear path for me when I put You first.

Thank You for Your words, which light my path, and for Your Holy Spirit, Who reveals to me Your plan for me. I treasure my life with and for You. Thank You, Father, for holding my future and me in the palm of Your hand.

In Jesus' name I pray. Amen.

---

### Scripture References

Deuteronomy 30:20

Psalms 25:5; 32:8;
  119:105

Proverbs 3:5,6; 4:18

Ecclesiastes 3:1-8

Isaiah 49:16

Jeremiah 33:3

John 16:13

Romans 8:14

1 Corinthians 2:9,10

Ephesians 1:16-18; 2:10

Philippians 4:11,13,19

Hebrews 13:5

1 Peter 5:7

## 23
## *Dedication of Your Tithes*

I profess this day unto the Lord God that I have come into the inheritance, which the Lord swore to give me. I am in the land that You have provided for me in Jesus Christ, the Kingdom of Almighty God. I was a sinner serving Satan; he was my god. But I called upon the name of Jesus, and You heard my cry and delivered me into the Kingdom of Your dear Son.

Jesus, my Lord and High Priest, I bring the firstfruits of my income to You and worship the Lord my God with them.

I rejoice in all the good, which You have given to my family and me. I have hearkened to the voice of the Lord my God and have done according to all that He has commanded me. Now look down from Your holy habitation from heaven and bless me as You said in Your Word. I thank You, Father, in Jesus' name. Amen.

### Scripture References

Deuteronomy 26:1,3,
 10,11,14,15 AMP
Colossians 1:13

Ephesians 2:1-5
Hebrews 3:1,7,8

## 24
## *To Live Free From Worry*

Father, I thank You that I have been delivered from the power of darkness and translated into the Kingdom of Your dear Son. I commit to live free from worry, in the name of Jesus, for the law of the Spirit of life in Christ Jesus has made me free from the law of sin and death.

I humble myself under Your mighty hand that in due time You may exalt me. I cast the whole of my cares (name them) — all my anxieties, all my worries, all my concerns, once and for all — on You. You care for me affectionately and care about me watchfully. You sustain me. You will never allow the consistently righteous to be moved — made to slip, fall, or fail!

Father, I delight myself in You, and You perfect that which concerns me. I cast down imaginations (reasonings) and every high thing that exalts itself against the knowledge of You, and bring into captivity every thought to the obedience of Christ.

I lay aside every weight and the sin of worry, which does try so easily to beset me. I run with patience the race that is set before me, looking unto Jesus, the Author and Finisher of my faith.

I thank You, Father, that You are able to keep that which I have committed unto You. I think on (fix my mind on) those things that are true, honest, just, pure, lovely, of good report, virtuous, and deserving of praise. I will not let my heart be troubled. I abide in Your Word, and Your Word abides in me. Father, I look into the perfect law of liberty and continue therein, being not a forgetful hearer, but a doer of the Word and thus blessed in my doing!

Thank You, Father. I am carefree. I walk in that peace which passes all understanding, in Jesus' name!

---

### Scripture References

Colossians 1:13

Romans 8:2

1 Peter 5:6,7 AMP

Psalms 37:4,5; 55:22; 138:8

2 Corinthians 10:5

Hebrews 12:1,2

2 Timothy 1:12

Philippians 4:6,8

John 14:1; 15:7

James 1:22-25

## 25
## *Peaceful Sleep*

Father, thank You for peaceful sleep, and for Your angels that encamp around us who fear You. You deliver us and keep us safe. The angels excel in strength and heed the voice of Your Word. You give Your angels charge over me, to keep me in all my ways.

I bring every thought, every imagination, and every dream into the captivity and obedience of Jesus Christ. Father, I thank You that even as I sleep, my heart counsels me and reveals to me Your purpose and plan. Thank You for sweet sleep, for You promise Your beloved sweet sleep. My heart is glad, and my spirit rejoices while my body and soul rest, confidently dwelling in safety. Amen.

### Scripture References

Psalms 16:7-9; 91:11;     Matthew 16:19; 18:18
   103:20; 127:2     2 Corinthians 10:5

Proverbs 3:24

## 26
## *Boyfriend/Girlfriend*

Father, I know that You care about every area of my life, especially whom I date. So I thank You for a friend who knows You, and is blessed with all spiritual blessings in Christ Jesus. Thank You that we will develop a true friendship while we are maturing, learning from one another, and having fun.

Father, thank You for the Holy Spirit Who reminds us to put You first while we develop a relationship that is pleasing to You. We will draw near to You, and You will draw near to us. We will resist the devil and he will flee from us. Thank You for bringing us together so we can encourage each other and grow closer to You, Father. I pray that we will stay on fire for You and love Jesus more and more, so that we can grow closer to You and minister to other people.

Knowing that unruly peers corrupt and
destroy good morals, help us to use good judgment and say no when we are pressured to go
places or behave contrary to Your will. I thank
You for the Holy Spirit, Who warns us of bad
situations and leads us into good situations.

Father, help us be doers of the Word. Help us
to treat each other with purity in our relationship, as brother and sister in the Lord. I pray
that our relationship will be a healthy one,
bringing growth and maturity to both of our
lives. And thank You that we have favor and a
good relationship with our families, because we
know that this is important to You. Help us just
to relax and develop our friendship.

Father, I pray that we will always listen to
Your voice and be sensitive to Your Spirit so
that we don't set ourselves up for a fall. Help
each of us establish sexual, physical, emotional,
and intellectual boundaries so we may walk, live,
and conduct ourselves in a manner worthy of
You. Thank You for Your angels who are
protecting us from all harm, evil, or danger.

Thank You for what You are doing in our lives. In Jesus' name I pray. Amen.

---

### *Scripture References*

Psalms 37:4; 91:11          Ephesians 1:3

John 14:18                  James 1:5,22

Romans 8:14                 1 Peter 5:7

1 Corinthians 15:33 AMP

## 27

## *Future Spouse*

Father, I seek first Your Kingdom and Your righteousness, and all things shall be added unto me. I know that You love me and that I can trust Your Word Who is Jesus, my Lord and Savior. I am in Him, made full and have come to the fullness of life. In Christ I am filled with the Godhead — Father, Son, and Holy Spirit — and reach full spiritual stature. And Christ is the Head of all rule and authority — of every angelic principality and power. Because of Jesus, I am complete; He is my Lord.

I come before You, Father, desiring a Christian mate. I petition that Your will be done in my life, and I enter into that blessed rest by adhering to, trusting in, and relying on You.

Father, You desire that I live a life free from care, that I should be content and satisfied in every situation that I am in, and that I should not be anxious or worried about anything. You have said that if I am willing and obedient to Your Word, You will give me the desires of my heart. It is my desire that someday I will be married to the person You have chosen for me.

I pray for my future spouse. Father, especially help each of us grow in love, Your kind of love. A friend loves at all times, and I desire for my spouse to be my very best friend. I desire that my spouse be a person who shares the same love that I have for You, someone who will be one in spirit and purpose with me.

I ask You to send mature men and women into our lives to give us good, godly counsel and to teach us how we should love each other and care for our family. Teach us both what You expect husbands and wives to do and how we ought to behave toward each other. Reveal to our hearts Your Word concerning the marriage relationship and correct any wrong thinking in our lives. Grant us knowledge through godly people, books, tapes, and preaching that will give us understanding concerning relationships, so that we can avoid damaging the relationship You desire for us.

Father, I trust You to lead me and guide me by Your Holy Spirit so that when Your perfect time arrives, I will have the wisdom, discretion, and discernment to know that my choice and Yours are the same for my life-mate. I am secure with the mind and the spirit that You have given me to make this decision.

Together we will build a godly home and fulfill Your purpose for the building of Your Kingdom. We will welcome each other's godly counsel, continually growing as we draw closer to You. In Jesus' name I pray. Amen.

### Scripture References

Philippians 2:2-7 KJV; 4:6,11 AMP

Colossians 1:9,10 KJV; 2:9,10 AMP

Genesis 2:18-24

Psalms 37:4,5; 130:5

Proverbs 17:17

Ephesians 5:22-25

Isaiah 1:19

Hebrews 4:3,10 AMP

Matthew 6:33 RSV

## 28

## *Victory Over Fear*

Father, when I am afraid, I will put my confidence in You. Yes, I will trust Your promises. And since I trust You, what can mere man do to me?

You have not given me a spirit of timidity, but of power and love and discipline (sound judgment). Therefore, I am not ashamed of the testimony of my Lord. I have not received a spirit of slavery leading to fear again, but I have received a spirit of adoption as a son, by which I cry out, "Abba! Father!"

Jesus, You delivered me, who, through fear of death, had been living all my life as a slave to constant dread. I receive the gift You left me — peace of mind and heart! And the peace You give isn't fragile like the peace the world gives. I cast away troubled thoughts, and I choose not to be afraid. I believe in God; I believe also in You.

Lord, You are my Light and my Salvation; You protect me from danger — whom shall I fear? When evil men come to destroy me, they will stumble and fall! Yes, though a mighty army marches against me, my heart shall know no fear! I am confident that You will save me.

Thank You, Holy Spirit, for bringing these things to my remembrance when I am tempted to be afraid. I will trust in my God. In the name of Jesus I pray. Amen.

---

### Scripture References

Psalms 27:1-3; 56:3-5 TLB    Hebrews 2:15 TLB

2 Timothy 1:7,8 NASB    John 14:1,17 TLB

Romans 8:15 NASB

## 29
## *Victory Over Pride*

Father, You hate a proud look; You resist the proud but give grace to the humble. In the name of Jesus, I submit to Your will for my life. I resist the devil, and he will flee from me. I renounce every manifestation of pride in my life as sin; I repent and turn from it.

As an act of faith, I clothe myself with humility and receive Your grace. I humble myself under Your mighty hand, Lord, that You may exalt me in due time. I refuse to exalt myself. I do not think of myself more highly than I ought; I do not have an exaggerated opinion of my own importance, but rate my ability with sober judgment, according to the degree of faith apportioned to me.

Proverbs 11:2 says, "When pride cometh, then cometh shame: but with the lowly is wisdom." Father, I set myself to resist pride when it comes. My desire is to be counted among the lowly, so I take on the attitude of a servant.

Father, You are faithful to dwell with one who is of a contrite and humble spirit. You revive the spirit of the humble and revive the heart of the contrite one. Thank You that the reward of humility and the reverent and worshipful fear of the Lord is riches and honor and life.

In Jesus' name I pray. Amen.

---

### Scripture References

Proverbs 6:16; 11:2; 21:4    Romans 12:3 AMP
Proverbs 22:4 AMP           Matthew 23:11
James 4:6,7                 Isaiah 57:15
1 Peter 5:5,6

## 30
# *Overcoming Intimidation*

Father, I come to You in the name of Jesus, confessing that intimidation has caused me to stumble. I ask Your forgiveness for thinking of myself as inferior, for I am created in Your image, and I am Your workmanship. Jesus said that the Kingdom of God is in me. Therefore, the power that raised Jesus from the dead dwells in me and causes me to face life with hope and divine energy.

The Lord is my Light and my Salvation; whom shall I fear? The Lord is the Strength of my life; of whom shall I be afraid? Lord, You said that You would never leave me or forsake me. Therefore, I can say without any doubt or fear that You are my Helper, and I am not afraid of anything that mere man can do to me. Greater is He that is in me than he that is in the world. If God is for me, who can be against me? I am free from the fear of man and public opinion.

Father, You have not given me a spirit of timidity — of cowardice, of craven and cringing and fawning fear — but You have given me a spirit of power and of love and of a calm and well-balanced mind and discipline and self-control. I can do all things through Christ, Who gives me the strength. Amen.

---

### Scripture References

| | |
|---|---|
| 1 John 1:9; 4:4 | 2 Timothy 1:7 |
| Luke 17:21 | Ephesians 1:19,20; 2:10 |
| Colossians 1:29 | Psalm 1:27 |
| Hebrews 13:5 | Proverbs 29:25 |
| Romans 3:31 | Philippians 4:13 |

## 31
### *Forgiveness When You Sin*

Father, I am sorry that I have sinned against
You. I believe that You are compassionate, slow
to anger, and filled with mercy and love, so I
run right to You and not away from You. I
confess my sin of _____, and ask
Your forgiveness. I don't deceive myself by
trying to say that I have not sinned.

Father, I repent and turn from my sin. I
determine with Your help to make restitution
when needed, and make necessary changes in
my life. Thank You for forgiving me and giving
me a pure heart and renewing a right spirit
within me. I am blessed because You have
removed my transgressions from me as far as
the east is from the west. You have removed the
weight of sin and lifted the burden of guilt that
has been weighing upon me. So by faith I
receive my forgiveness.

In Jesus' name I pray. Amen.

---

### *Scripture References*

| | |
|---|---|
| Psalms 32:1,2; 51:10,17 | Romans 6:13,14 |
| Psalm 103:2-4,8, | Philippians 2:5,13 |
| 11-13 AMP | Colossians 2:13,14 AMP |
| Proverbs 28:13 | Hebrews 1:9; 4:16; 12:1 |
| Acts 26:20 | 1 John 1:8-10 |

## 32
## *Abstinence From Premarital Sex*

Father, in view of Your mercy, I offer my body as a living sacrifice, holy and pleasing to You — this is my spiritual act of worship. I will not copy the sexual behavior and customs of this world.

Sexual sin is never right. No other sin affects the body as this one does. This sin is against my own body. My body is not meant for sexual immorality, but for You, and You for the body.

My body is the temple of the Holy Spirit. I am not my own, but You have bought me with a great price. I use every part of my body to bring glory to You because my body belongs to You.

In Jesus' name I pray. Amen.

### Scripture References

Psalm 119:9

Romans 6:13,14; 8:5,6

Romans 12:1,2 TLB

James 1:22

1 Corinthians 10:13

1 Corinthians 6:18-20;
  9:22 TLB

1 Thessalonians 4:4;
  5:22,23

1 Peter 1:18,19

## 33
## *Alcohol/Drug/Tobacco Addiction*

Father, in the mighty name of Jesus, I come boldly to Your throne of grace that I may obtain mercy and find grace to help in my time of need. I ask forgiveness for rebelling against You, my parents, teachers, policemen, and against myself. I need Your deliverance and protection from every evil.

Lord, I want to be free from alcohol/drugs/tobacco, but I can't do it alone; I need Your help. I believe Your Word, and that truth will set me free, because since Jesus has made me free, I am free indeed. I need Your help to overcome temptation. Give me the grace I need to walk in the Spirit, so I won't fulfill the lusts of the flesh. Help me to control my thoughts. Keep me from willful sins. May they not rule over me. Father, You are faithful. You will not allow me to be tempted beyond my powers of endurance. In every temptation You will always show me a way out. I determine not to go to the wrong types of parties or places that will make it easier to give in to alcohol/drugs/tobacco.

I will renew my mind by reading Your Word so that I can change the way I think and be set free from bad habits and from the lies that I have believed. I know that You will change my desires, Father, when I delight myself in You. Thank You that I have been freed from my sin by the blood of Jesus.

Thank You for forgiving me and for forgetting the sins of my past. I look to You for a great, new future. It is a new day! I am a new person — I am a new creation in Christ Jesus.

Thank You, Lord, for a life free from rebellion and addictions. Please guide me to a godly counselor, friend, or support group. Thank You that You are giving me good habits where I once had bad habits. In Jesus' name I pray. Amen.

### *Scripture References*

Psalms 19:13; 37:4-6;
   103:11-14
Hebrews 4:14-16
John 8:32,36
2 Peter 2:9
1 Corinthians 15:33,34
Isaiah 43:18,19

2 Timothy 4:18
Galatians 5:18-21
Romans 13:14
1 Corinthians 10:13
   PHILLIPS
Jeremiah 29:11
2 Corinthians 5:17

## 34
## *When You Feel Lonely or Unloved*

Father, when other people leave me and I feel unloved, I am thankful that You will never, ever leave me alone or reject me. You are a help for me in this time of loneliness. I know that Your angels are all around me.

You are my God. I know that You love me. Jesus even gave His life for me. I am a born-again Christian, Jesus lives in my heart, and I am on my way to heaven. That is plenty to be thankful for. So I won't allow myself to be discouraged or feel sorry for myself. I choose to think only on those things that are pure, holy, and good, even when I am alone.

Although I may feel alone, I am not alone, for Your Word says that there is nothing that can separate me from the love of Christ. I will come out on top of every circumstance through Jesus' love.

In Jesus' name I pray. Amen.

---

### *Scripture References*

John 16:32; 8:35,37;          Psalms 34:7; 37:4; 46:1
   10:9,10; 12:21          Ephesians 4:31,32; 5:1,2
Deuteronomy 31:8          John 3:16; 16:32
1 Samuel 30:6          Philippians 4:8

## 35
## *American Government*

Father, in Jesus' name, we give thanks for the United States and its government. We pray and intercede for the leaders in our land: the president, the representatives, the senators, the judges, the governors, the mayors, the police officers, and all those in authority over us in any way. We pray that the Spirit of the Lord rests upon them.

We believe that skillful and godly wisdom has entered into the heart of our president and knowledge is pleasant to him. Discretion watches over him; understanding keeps him and delivers him from evil.

Father, we ask that You encircle the president with people who make their hearts and ears attentive to godly counsel and do right in Your sight. We believe You cause them to be people of integrity who are obedient concerning us, that we may lead a quiet and peaceable life in all godliness and honesty. We pray that the upright shall dwell in our government — that leaders blameless and complete in Your sight shall remain but the wicked shall be cut off and the treacherous rooted out.

Your Word declares that "blessed is the nation whose God is the Lord" (Ps. 33:12). We receive Your blessing. Father, You are our Refuge and Stronghold in times of trouble (high cost, destitution, and desperation). So we declare with our mouths that Your people dwell safely in this land, and we *prosper* abundantly. We are more than conquerors through Christ Jesus!

It is written in Your Word that the heart of the king is in the hand of the Lord, and You turn it whichever way You desire. We believe the heart of our leader is in Your hand and that his decisions are directed of the Lord.

We give thanks unto You that the good news of the Gospel is published in our land. The Word of the Lord prevails and grows mightily in the hearts and lives of the people. We give thanks for this land and the leaders You have given to us, in Jesus' name.

*Jesus is Lord over the United States! Amen.*

---

### Scripture References

1 Timothy 2:1-3

Proverbs 2:10-12,21,22; 21:1

Psalms 9:9; 33:12

Deuteronomy 28:10,11

Romans 8:37 AMP

Acts 12:24

# *Prayer of Salvation*

God loves you—no matter who you are, no matter what your past. God loves you so much that He gave His one and only begotten Son for you. The Bible tells us, "...whoever believes in him shall not perish but have eternal life" (John 3:16 NIV). Jesus laid down His life and rose again so that we could spend eternity with Him in heaven and experience His absolute best on earth. If you would like to receive Jesus into your life, say the following prayer out loud and mean it from your heart.

*Heavenly Father, I come to You admitting that I am a sinner. Right now, I choose to turn away from sin, and I ask You to cleanse me of all unrighteousness. I believe that Your Son, Jesus, died on the cross to take away my sins. I also believe that He rose again from the dead so that I might be forgiven of my sins and made righteous through faith in Him. I call upon the name of Jesus Christ to be the Savior and Lord of my life. Jesus, I choose to follow You and ask that You fill me with the power of the Holy Spirit. I declare that right now I am a child of God. I am free from sin and full of the righteousness of God. I am saved in Jesus' name. Amen.*

If you prayed this prayer to receive Jesus Christ as your Savior for the first time, please contact us on the Web at **www.harrisonhouse.com** to receive a free book.

Or you may write to us at
**Harrison House**
P.O. Box 35035
Tulsa, Oklahoma 74153

## *About the Author*

Germaine Griffin Copeland, is the bestselling author of the *Prayers That Avail Much*® family of books. The books are now in several languages, and there are more than three million copies in print.

She is the daughter of the late Reverend A. H. "Buck" and Donnis Brock Griffin. Germaine lives with her husband, Everette, in Roswell, Georgia. They have four children, ten grandchildren, and five great-grandchildren.

## *MISSION STATEMENT*
### *Word Ministries, Inc.*

To motivate individuals to spiritual growth
and emotional wholeness,
encouraging them to become more deeply
and intimately acquainted
with the Father God
as they pray prayers that avail much.


You may contact Word Ministries by writing
**Word Ministries, Inc.**
38 Sloan Street
Roswell, Georgia 30075
or calling 770-518-1065
www.prayers.org

*Please include your testimonies
and praise reports when you write.*

# Other Books by Germaine Copeland

Additional copies of this book are
available at your local bookstore.

**HARRISON HOUSE**
Tulsa, Oklahoma 74153

# www.harrisonhouse.com

### *Fast. Easy. Convenient!*

- ◆ New Book Information
- ◆ Look Inside the Book
- ◆ Press Releases
- ◆ Bestsellers

- ◆ Free E-News
- ◆ Author Biographies
- ◆ Upcoming Books
- ◆ Share Your Testimony

For the latest in book news and author information, please visit us on the Web at www.harrisonhouse.com. Get up-to-date pictures and details on all our powerful and life-changing products. Sign up for our e-mail newsletter, *Friends of the House,* and receive free monthly information on our authors and products including testimonials, author announcements, and more!

Harrison House—

*Books That Bring Hope, Books That Bring Change*

## *More Prayers That Avail Much!*

 If this book has been a blessing to you, these dynamic prayers are available in their entirety in the clothbound edition of *Prayers That Avail Much®*. Check with your local bookstore or visit us at www.harrisonhouse.com. *Prayers That Avail Much for Women* — ISBN 1-57794-489-5

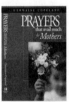

*Prayers That Avail Much for Mothers*
ISBN 1-57794-490-9

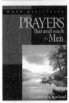

*Prayers That Avail Much for Men*
ISBN 1-57794-182-9

*Prayers That Avail Much for Teens*
ISBN 1-57794-491-7

*The Harrison House Vision*

Proclaiming the truth and the power

Of the Gospel of Jesus Christ

With excellence;

Challenging Christians to

Live victoriously,

Grow spiritually,

Know God intimately.